For John
from Joseph Solman

JOSEPH SOLMAN

JOSEPH SOLMAN

Introduction by A. L. Chanin • DOCENT, MUSEUM OF MODERN ART

CROWN PUBLISHERS, INC. · NEW YORK, N.Y.

FRONTISPIECE:
Diagonals. 1940. Oil, 12 x 20 in.
Dr. and Mrs. D. Epstein, New York

© 1966 by Joseph Solman
Published by Crown Publishers, Inc., New York, N.Y.
Library of Congress Catalog Card Number: 66-15519
Printed in the U.S.A.

Produced under the supervision of Gerald M. Konecky
by Graphic Offset Co., Inc., New York, N.Y.
Designed by Klaus Gemming
Photos (black and white) by Walter Rosenblum, Aaron Siskind,
Bernard Cole, John Schiff, and (color) by Mel Levine

The Art of Joseph Solman

A. L. CHANIN

Joseph Solman's art evolved during the tumultuous Thirties when American painting like American life, was an encounter of outworn and newly emerging ideas.

The sum of a Solman painting is in its uncommon color ensembles, a simplicity that veils highly complex relationships of design, an eloquence of rhythm, and an unusually sensitive and animate line. His art, delicate in surface, is inwardly firm and architectural. He explores relatively few themes; city scenes, studio interiors, still lifes and portraits. The cityscapes are broadly simplified yet suffused with the sense of locale. His well-known interiors, sparse and at once full, contain a variety of spatial arrangements. His long series of portraits are by turn warm and intimate, wry and penetrating, and often memorable both as design and delineation. His imagination is sparked by a chair, a window or a broom; a street sign becomes both description and enigma. As Solman draws inner fire from commonplace objects and forms, he distills their elements into arresting designs.

His invention does not flag in repeating a motif. Like Giacometti or Morandi, Solman believes mystery and depth can be sustained by exploring a small, cherished corner of his world. His themes recall Degas' remark, "one must do the same object over and over again, ten times, no a hundred. Nothing in art should resemble an accident, not even movement." His considerable technical skill is full of understatement. And if it is an art of balance and lucidity, it is equally an art of true passion.

Like so many artists whose work embodies deeply-felt aspects of America, Solman was born in Europe; in Vitebsk, Russia, in 1909, the son of a tailor. The family migrated to America in 1912, and settled in Jamaica, Long Island. Young Solman sketched incessantly, with pencil or chalk: "My mother used to declare that I drew at the crawling stage. Unlike sensible children, I continued indefinitely...There was no question in my mind by the age of thirteen that I was going to be a painter." This innate love of drawing, plus his gift for portraiture, earned the youngster early satisfaction. "In High School [Jamaica High School] I had ample opportunity to revenge myself on teachers I disliked by publishing caricatures of them in the student magazine. They even sat eagerly for my drawings."

In 1926, at the age of seventeen, Solman enrolled at the National Academy of Design, attending evening sessions, chiefly under the skillful portraitist, Ivan G. Olinsky. During the day he worked as a bookkeeper. And on the long subway journey to and from

Pencil Sketch. 1926. *Pencil Sketch.* 1929.

school (then on West 109th Street) he sketched the passengers again and again. "It gave me a far better training in the figure than I ever achieved at the Academy alone." Among his classmates were Herman Rose, the late Byron Browne and Ilya Bolotowsky—artists with whom he would later exhibit on a number of occasions.

Soon the ultra-conservative instruction cooled his ardor. He left the Academy and—like all artists—became his own teacher. He rented a studio of his own, and supported himself by shifting to night jobs—running an elevator in an apartment house, or working at a soda fountain. His older brother, an electrician, shared his studio, giving warm encouragement to the young artist.

Among Solman's earliest enthusiasms were the American portrait and genre painters, Frank Duveneck, Jerome Myers and George Luks. Hours spent in the Metropolitan Museum, before some Rembrandts, were eventually more rewarding. Another experience was the discovery, through a book of reproductions, of the compact power and rude grandeur of Daumier. Also significant in terms of his early development were the mystical oils of Ryder; and, naturally, echoes of Daumier, Rembrandt and Ryder appear in his work at this period (see plate 1, "Meyer").

These tyro ventures were soon to give way to far more mature and personal paintings. The probing for new expression came, in part, from contact with masterpieces of nineteenth and twentieth century European art. There were exhibitions at the Museum of Modern Art, beginning with the memorable opening exhibition of Cézanne, van Gogh, Gauguin and Seurat; and the fine Gallatin Collection, now in the Philadelphia Museum; but earlier, on loan at New York University.

Solman was courting his future wife, Ruth Romanofsky, a journalism student at N.Y.U., and here he became acquainted with Gallatin's key pictures by Picasso, Leger, Braque,

Miró, Klee and Kandinsky. (Klee's "Landscape with Blue Birds" was an especial favorite and today the Solmans own a small but fine group of Klees, collected, bit by bit, over the years. They also have a superb Daumier drawing, and noteworthy examples by Klimt, Pascin and Moore.)

It was therefore a question of only two or three years for Solman to discard Duveneck for masters like Cézanne and Klee. And so about 1930, he started a long series of small gouaches in which elements of cubism, flat space, and dark expressionist moods were partially peppered. His motifs were the streets, alleys and railroad yards of South Jamaica (see plates 2, 3, 4, 5).

In 1931, Solman hopefully exhibited about a dozen of these in a Washington Square show—at a time when this outdoor art display offered the public more serious fare. His pictures attracted Joseph Kling, who ran then, as now, the Village's International Book and Art Shop. Kling bought several gouaches. The following year the Jumble Shop, a Village landmark, hung several in a group show selected by a jury. Solman was told that the jury of three, including Reginald Marsh and Guy Pêne du Bois, was enthusiastic about his entries. "For years thereafter it was the warm praise of fellow artists that encouraged me during the long no-sale period."

During the Depression, in 1933, Solman married Ruth. They have a son and daughter, Paul and Ronni. Husband and wife both worked part-time at Kling's book and art shop. In April of the following year (1934) Solman held his first one-man show at the Contemporary Arts Gallery, directed by Miss Emily Francis, who dedicated her place to first solo shows by promising artists. Mark Tobey, Earl Kerkam and John Kane were among those given their introductory exhibitions by the tireless Miss Francis. The catalogue stated that "Mr. Solman has an insatiable curiosity amounting to a passion, for old, grim streets." Indeed, most of the compositions were the visions of a somewhat melancholy stroller with, here and there, a too-ardent homage to Ryder and Rouault.

Margaret Breuning of *The Sun* remarked, grumpily, "...still another celebrant of gloom...." but added, "his work seems marked by a genuine feeling and once your eyes adapt themselves to his lowered scale you will find it shot through with smouldering color, vague and haunting." "Later," recalls the artist, "I was to kick my foot through many of these

Sid. 1928.

dark, scabrous canvases. A very healthy feeling, by the way...." Perhaps these pictures reflected in part the precarious existence of a newly married artist.

But a new period was about to begin, thanks to the creative initiative of the government art projects. From 1935 to 1941, Solman was employed on the W.P.A. art project at $21.50 a week. Thus he and other artists could concentrate on painting—despite the oppressive news and the increasingly ominous headlines about Hitler and Mussolini. His work now had a maximum opportunity to proliferate. City streets, old storefronts, harbors, parks, ice cellars, portraits of friends and still lifes followed one another in profusion.

The best of the city scenes were shown in 1937, his second one-man show, in a gallery organized by the late de Hirsch Margulies, colorful village character and talented watercolorist. The gallery, jauntily called "Another Place," was a forerunner of the current "off-Broadway" galleries. The show received friendly and perceptive reviews. Under the title, "Solman: Striking Pattern and Subject Matter," *Art News* wrote of Solman as "fascinated by those symbols of trade and industry which are hung over doorways."

Among these canvases, *Venus of 23rd Street*, a hypnotic medley of shapes and signs, (see plate 7) is a prime example of Solman's street period; made up of traffic signals, barber pole and a signboard of a nude strapped in surgical appliances. As she presides over the scene she takes on something of the enigmatic quality of the symbols in a Chirico or Klee. The lively array of street forms is chiefly vertical, set against the flat sky; and anchored below by the converging thrust of the pavement and the stark green shadow.

The rich group of objects is selected from the chaos of realism and sharply compressed. For example, the red traffic light which accentuates space is echoed in the stripes of the barber pole; which in turn is linked as well as contrasted with the stripes of the awning. To the left, the railing of the El is balanced by the structure of the fire-escape. It is interesting to note that, unlike Chirico's hushed streets, nothing has been placed out of context. On the contrary, everything is its own familiar self, yet a real sense of mystery is projected.

This power to arrest the eye and mind by selecting and composing the hybrid elements of a street is also present in *The Bootblack Shop* (see plate 20) and *The Oculist* (see plate 8). Here Solman distorts the architecture to stress the swift, swaying movement of an El train. The lines of the El, like those of the buildings on the right lead to the climax of the *Daily News* skyscraper. Once more the contrasting image is the Oculist's sign, a huge eye, which startles the street.

As in *Venus of 23rd Street*, no people stroll or throng the streets. Nevertheless, these scenes are instinct with a sense of their presence. The effect in both paintings is of a vivid stage-set, a moment before it springs to life with actors.

In *Ice Cellar* (see plate 27), there is a greater control in the device of flattening form; and a Klee-like delight in the repertoire of letters and arrows. Among the last of the paintings of New York scenes, *Madison Square Park* (see plate 17) incorporates figures, bushes and trees as a foil to the silhouetted statue of Seward. The patch of green grass acts as a bridge between the two clusters of people, and the waste can, with its forlorn umbrella, echoes the impassive dignity of the sculpture.

Shortly before his second exhibition, Solman had become a member of an unusual group, *The Ten*. Obviously he had long since passed the stage of an individual groping for a point of view. As his understanding of the art movements around him clarified, he looked for a gallery with a definite creed, or principles, rather than a gallery that chose, in a haphazard way, personal favorites.

In 1936, when Robert Godsoe opened the Secession Gallery in the Village, he invited a number of talented artists, expressionist and abstract, who were without a regular place, including Byron Browne, Balcomb Greene, and many others. However, the Gallery was eventually overrun with too many painters, "and a group of us seceded from Secession." They formed *The Ten*. The original group consisted of Ben-Zion, Adolph Gottlieb, Mark Rothko, Jankel Kufeld, Ilya Bolotowsky, Louis Harris, Louis Schanker, Tschacbasov and Solman. Afterwards, Ralph Rosenborg, Earl Kerkam and John Graham were members.

The art of *The Ten* varied in style, but all struck a challenging note. Critics were startled and intrigued: "Expressionism is relaunched by *The Ten*." Henry McBride declared "These young artists are completely uninhibited...They attack a canvas with as much fury and excitement as they would spend if attacking a government. Some of them have already said, 'Down with subject matter!' and have become cubists. Some of them go into trances and paint dreams. Some of them mock politicians....They dare any theme, and in a splashing, dashing, youthful fashion get away with it."

In November 1938, *The Ten* staged a significant protest exhibition against what they considered the routine, dogmatic academicism of the Whitney's Annual. The dissenters, who had refused to submit to the giant show, decried "the reputed equivalence of American painting and literal painting." They declared that "the symbol of the silo is in the ascendant at our Whitney Museum of Modern Art."

"Most critics," recalled Solman, "labelled us dirty expressionists. The term expressionist was aesthetically subversive at the time. The art climate was predominantly Woodstock (Alexander Brook), social protest (Shahn and the Mexicans) and American westerns (Benton, Curry and Wood). We were outcasts on the scene, only John Marin and Max Weber, and to a smaller extent Stuart Davis, Hartley, Knaths and Avery were tolerated as representative of the growing modern tradition. Though the pressures of individuality finally broke up our group in 1941, we had given each other heart for a valuable period of time. We had been toughened and scarred in the art arena and remained undaunted thereafter..."

Solman's work now caught the appraising notice of one of the few authentically creative dealers in modern art in this city, the late J. B. Neumann. He invited the artist to join his New Art Circle. The young artist was proud to have his work hung alongside Klee, Beckmann, and Rouault, Europeans who were first introduced to the American public via J. B.'s gallery. In a 1938 group exhibition, "Five New American Painters," he showed Solman's work, together with Lee Gatch, Earl Kerkam, Karl Knaths and Joseph di Martini. Then he included Solman in a three-man show with Rothko and Marcel Gromaire. Also during this period Solman helped to edit together with Meyer Shapiro and Harold Rosenberg, *Art Front*, the Journal of the Artists' Union. Shortly afterwards, he was sent by the Art Project Administration to the Spokane Art Center to teach and organize exhibitions. The relatively quiet atmosphere of the West resulted in several interiors, the start of a notable series (see plate 32).

On returning to his large loft studio in New York he pursued the more intimate style of the "interiors," using a corner of the studio with a half-opened ceiling window cutting varied geometric patterns of light and shadow.

Thirty paintings, the result of several years of intense, stimulating work—were shown in a large exhibit, at the Bonestell Gallery in 1942. One room was given over to portraits, one to interiors, another to still lifes. Collector Sidney Janis, later to become a leading dealer, wrote the foreword to the catalogue, "the still lifes, interiors and portrait studies included in the present exhibition reflect moments of quiet inner serenity. Originally, vibrating exteriors came from the brush of Solman. Between these phases there is no sharp break for they are part of a cycle yet to be completed...." His style, said Janis, "was neither abstract nor expressionist but rather a fusion of the two...."

An example of this period, *Diagonals*, (see frontispiece) is a small, compact canvas full of subtleties. A cool, olive-green zone of light on the window repeats the triangles of light on the wall, ledge and floor. The Seurat print and the building across the way blunt the play of diagonals.

Duncan Phillips bought several oils and planned an exhibition at his notable museum of modern art in Washington, D.C., the Phillips' Memorial Gallery. Unfortunately, a trucking strike postponed this, but seven years later, in 1949, Phillips gave Solman a large retrospective.

Then, early in 1941, Solman received an offer of an odd, "temporary" job from his brother-in-law, as a pari-mutuel ticket clerk at the New York racetracks. The art projects were ending with America's deepening involvement in the war, so Solman decided to try it. He said, "It payed the lucrative wage of $8.00 per day for what amounted to an afternoon's work, and it left me free for a full six months of painting. It was a new world to me, a mild, fenced-off, lunatic asylum with Damon Runyon characters and picturesque chatter....Before the season was out, I could 'dope out' horses from the *Morning Telegraph* as well as the best handicapper with the same disastrous results." Aside from economic help, the job resulted in one of his finest portraits—indeed, one of the finest of contemporary American portraits, *Eddie* (see plate 88) and, later, a series of vivid sketches on newspaper made during the subway rides to and from the track.

After Pearl Harbor Solman worked in defense, in New Jersey shipyards and as an isometric draftsman for Pratt and Whitney Aircraft. In the evenings, as a relief from the dry precision of his work, he embarked on a long-cherished project—"imaginative sketches of my idol in music, Mozart." From among more than thirty varied watercolors of the Olympian composer's profile, Solman, with the expert help of Leonard Pytlak, silk-screened the twelve finest. Some of the silk-screens employed as many as 16 different colors. Elegant and linear in diagram, the portraits range from the droll to the

Subway Sketch. 1928.   *Subway Sketch.* 1961.

intimate and abstract. The folio was published in an edition of 200 and exhibited at the Bonestell Gallery in 1945 (see plates 45, 46, 47, 48). About this time, the large oil, *Red Semaphore*, included in the Metropolitan Museum's *Artists for Victory* exhibition, was purchased by the Pepsi-Cola Company (see plate 21).

From 1944 to 1952, the Solmans lived in the huge Knickerbocker Village development near the East River. He worked again at the racetrack during the Spring and Summer season and painted in the Fall and Winter. Here a large basement room became his studio as well as the raw material for some exceptional paintings, the well-known series of interiors. It was here that he elaborated so many of them, based on the mullioned windows, a waste can, broom, chairs, and the general litter of a studio; based, too, as Solman observed "on the divine daylight filtering through the windows that can make the merest dustpan or bottle a hushed and holy object." The series marks a high point in Solman's art, not only in a deepening quality but in a greater resourcefulness with paint.

In a perceptive article by Dorothy Seckler in *Art News* (August 1951), "Solman Paints a Picture," in which the development of *Blue Interior* (see plate 77) is given in detail, the critic wrote: "The atmosphere of Solman's studio, which others might find gloomy, offers the artist a needed retreat...if the shadowy recesses and their tumbled content are like Chardin, the window area, embracing the length of the large rectangular room, provides a more modern aspect. Immediately familiar through his paintings are the varied tiers, with rhythmically changing divisions. Again and again they have provided a proscenium vast in scale in relation to his small objects, a backdrop of light most often keyed to the reticent blues and greens which predominate in the winter months but in summer mornings assuming a rosy or golden ambience." And, after discussing the various steps in the construction of *Blue Interior*, Seckler concluded, "It was amazing to see how early distortions had been absorbed into the structure, strengthening its underlying architecture and lending a suppressed animation to every object."

From his large exhibition at the Phillips Memorial Gallery in 1949, the museum added two more Solmans to their collection. One of these, *The Broom* (see plate 68) exploits with Degas-like ingenuity the disposition of space in the large areas of floor and wall. Once more, the homely cast of characters appears; chair, canvas, bottle and broom, whose long handle provides the only diagonal shift from the sequence of uprights. An ivory-like glow illuminates the room. As in the street scenes, everything seems to wait expectantly for the human presence.

With a more dramatic emphasis, *The Studio* of 1948 (see plate 69) in the Brandeis University collection, places a mug, teapot, dustpan, broom and canvas into a setting of golden chrome greens. With miserly caution, Solman distributes his richly telling accents. In *Interior With Statue* (see plate 60) in the Hirschhorn collection, lines sway and tilt across a daring composition of horizontals. The insistent but varied rectangles of the window, the waste can, a spindly stool, the canvas stretcher, all fuse in a slow-paced choreography; enlivened by the chalk white of a sculpture and the bright red of a bookjacket. Each object, like "group acting," gradually loses its seeming isolation to play a carefully plotted role in this subterranean drama.

The 1949 *Interior with Green Wall* (see plate 78) ranks with the finest of Solman's compositions. In it he creates tension by varying the effect of flat surfaces versus modelled areas. Again, affectionate response to the prosaic comes through with eloquence; especially in the cunning sequence of the curtains across the wall. The tilted canvas on the sculptor's stand and the high stool are given an awkward grace in keeping with the flutter and drifting movement of the drapes. Anchoring everything is the solid turquoise wall.

In *Regards From Chicago* (see plate 54) the objects form a counterpoint of diagonal movements, climaxed by a vermillion pencil. The postcard, from which the title derives, echoes the old signboards in his street scenes. Again, each object is seen freshly—even a routine ink-bottle becomes an austere shape.

In 1950, Solman joined the A.C.A. Gallery, well-known for its social scene painters. His one-man show there, featuring some of his best interiors, drew important response from the press and the art public. Stuart Preston in the *Times* spoke of the "light" as "principally a means of forcing the spectator to discover strange beauties in unpromising places...there is also a note of strangeness in the absence of all figures when everything speaks of the human presence." In speaking of "the distinguished portraits" Preston particularly noted "the pathos of Eddie." This was a reference to the portrait of a racetrack colleague that Solman had exhibited some time earlier in a group show with Evergood and Moses Soyer.

My own column in the *Compass*, reviewing the exhibition, spotlighted this brilliant portrayal: "Departing from his usual variations on the theme of interiors, Solman also contributes one of the most incisive and penetrating portraits I have seen recently—the *Portrait of Eddie*. Expressed in terms of color and pattern, with the striped suit and necktie playing an important role in the total design, Solman catches the lean, sharp, alert mood of a racetrack employee; the sporting page comes alive in paint" (see plate 88).

In 1941, Solman had already painted one of his most forceful portraits, *Ruth*, the artist's wife, a brooding and dramatic work (see plate 18). The face is strongly modelled in unorthodox color—dark green—in contrast to the bright floral patterns of the robe.

Eddie's portrait and several more betokened a shift back to his first love, the portrait, just at the time when his interiors began to attract wide attention. "I decided to probe portraiture again" the artist said, "only when I felt free to use the face and figure in any color, shape or form that I wished." He worked intensively between 1950-1955, using his friends as sitters.

The idea of a solo exhibition devoted completely to serious portraits seemed so startling, outdated, or futile that Solman softened the blow with a droll preface to his December 1954 exhibition: "A writer friend of mine was working away at a novel for some months when his indulgent grandmother finally asked him what he was doing alone in his room all that time. 'I'm writing,' he answered. 'To whom?' she asked, beamingly.

"Colleagues have asked what I've been painting these days and upon hearing 'portraits' have added 'commissions, I suppose.' This is, of course, a commentary on the state of portraiture today, which in the main, has been left to the academic and commercial markets.

It was not primarily the camera that clicked away the centuries-old tradition of probing the human face in paint. Degas, Manet, van Gogh and Eakins all worked long after the advent of photography. But many of the recent art movements, with their ceaseless experimentation, have relegated subject to a secondary role or obliterated it entirely. Munch, Sickert, Vuillard, Modigliani and Kokoschka are among the exceptions who have kept the mainstream of portraiture alive. Sutherland in England has made an honest effort to return to it. I hope we may one day see it as a living force again in our country."

Larry Campbell, in *Art News*, wrote of Solman's portraits enthusiastically: "It is supposed that it is impossible to be true both to sitter and to the demands of modern painting. But a reconciliation between the two can be made, and this strong exhibition shows how... the paint itself was applied to establish its own particular rhythms—complementing the others so that when examined under a magnifying glass every inch is transformed into little glowing abstractions. Apart from his ability to get a compelling likeness... and the formal and human aspect of his work, it is the haunting color varying from local to atmospheric and synthetic, that makes the show memorable."

Larry Rivers, at this time, also held an exhibition of portraits, at the De Nagy Gallery. Preston in the *New York Times* stated: "Not all modern artists have joined the headlong flight from reality.... Two current exhibitors, both, incidentally, of portraits, the most humanistic art form, are points of proof. Joseph Solman and Larry Rivers are irreproachably modern painters and yet for them, paradox though it may seem, art is more visually inspired than it is intellectually...." And after a lengthy description of their work, concluded, "with work of this quality these two artists promise to rescue portraiture from its recent doldrums."

An entire show of portraits scarcely offered any possibility of sales, but Ella and the late Herman Baron of the A.C.A. backed up Solman wholeheartedly. When the exhibition proved a hit, all three were surprised. Four portraits were immediately acquired by Joseph Hirschhorn. Half a dozen more went to other collectors and casual visitors. The artist had the feeling that the public understood them primarily as "paintings."

The show's success finally enabled Solman to see the European museums. In 1956, he and his family travelled through France, Holland and Italy. "I drank in my museums to the full. I had waited many years for this journey. Ingres in the Louvre, Tintoretto in Venice and Rembrandt at the National Gallery gave me fond permission to continue my portraiture...."

Among Solman's portraits, those of the late Byron Browne, and his wife, Rosalind, form a distinguished pair. In the first (see plate 82) a supple line emphasizes the solidity of the sitter. The intricate planes of the face are opposed to a relatively flat rendering of the shirt, tie and setting of a room, and all the subtleties of line, color and space are used to reinforce the sitter's personality.

The main scheme of *Rosalind* (see plate 119) is, naturally, more curvelinear. Sweeping contour lines create a decorative boundary to the vivid blue and green of the dress. Lines join at pivotal junctures, then separate, thus defining both interrelated *and* independent areas, a fine example of Solman's gift for shape-making.

For a while in 1956-1957, Solman's feeling for bold patterns resulted in a brown-tan period, almost woodcut-like in manner (see plates 109, 110, 111). Then he found the lean diet too severe for him, though it affected a few later works, notably the brilliant *Pushcart* of 1960 (see plate 116), as well as a 1958 portrait of *Angela* (see plate 113). This work is keyed to a few notes of browns and blue-greys. Her character is evoked not only by this Spartan color scheme but by an incisive line which traces the stoical dignity of her face.

Several more exhibitions of portraits followed, and his 1961 show at the Crystal Gallery was well received. "But," said Solman, "the tide of abstraction and metaphysics was reaching its height." In Solman's words, "...promoting names and encouraging large-scale canvases was the order of the day; the museums were calling the tune and too many artists were dancing to it. The Salon days were here again in modern dress. Nevertheless, I continued to paint portraits. And in 1961, I won the $2,000. National Institute of Arts and Letters award, along with Prestopino, Murch and Cadmus. It was the only prize I ever received. It spoiled a perfect record."

In 1960, he made an idle pencil drawing in the *Morning Telegraph* newspaper while on the subway going to the track. "It was quite by accident as I had no sketch pad with me and I was excited by a subject. I mounted the sketch and tried to obliterate the print with gouache to leave the pencil line clear. I then tried a few in color. The result turned into a long series of "subway riders," the train a marvellous studio where every type in the world may sit for you, weary old travellers, dapper executives and 'teased-hair' sirens." One of the chief implements of Solman's art, his expressive "bent-wire" line, provides the essence of these lively sketches. Both in these studies, and in his oils where he reveals the skeleton of a chair or the intricacy of an eye-socket, Solman possesses the quality of an innate draughtsman.

His 1961 show also presented several studies of young "beats." They were the first of a remarkable series of characterizations which opened up a new world for the painter, enriching his style in the process. His neighborhood on East Tenth Street had become the East Village, swarming with young couples, writers, actors, dancers and artists, clothed in their unorthodox fashion. For the last several years Solman has concentrated on portraying them. One result is a departure in technique. Instead of overlays of solid impasto or minute pigment variations, large washes of color thinned with turpentine are broadly applied on the white canvas. The aim is a fusion of shape, drawing and color into one spontaneous impression. "I wish to emphasize," he says, "that I begin and complete all my works with the subject before me...I have long discovered for *myself* that what we call the subject yields more pattern, more poetry, more drama, greater abstract design and tension than any shapes we may invent."

East Village Couple (see plate 126) is outstanding among these recent portrayals. Its controlled but fluid intensity underlines the strange relationship of the sitters. The faces, though highly individual, also become representative types. In this picture, gesture is as important as dress, color as revealing as physiognomy, mood as fundamental as the massing of forms.

Mother and Child. 1962.   *Reading the Form.* 1964.

In another striking characterization, *Margie* (see plate 127) slouches in a chair, her head simply and deftly handled with maroon hair framing the oval of a wary face. Her typical blue duffel coat merging in a cataract of paint with her blue stockings carries the eye across the length of the canvas. The painter catches a touch of swagger in the coat which fixes her allegiance to her "in" group.

Thus in the 1960's, Solman has achieved a personal renaissance. These recent oils form an absorbing portrait gallery of The Scene. What is quite surprising is that these faces, tense or brooding, with their casually defiant attire, have so far largely escaped the notice of other painters. Into these portraits he has infused the sympathetic perception of a man, who, once a rebel himself, has a deep interest in these young non-conformists.

The new pictures reveal the artist's delight in working with these exciting forms, faces and figures. Solman's art, spanning more than thirty years of reflective and poetic painting, thirty years of the kind of integrity that snubs the merely fashionable, may well survive and outdistance some of the more publicized painters of the last three decades.

1. *Meyer.* 1930. Oil, 15 x 19 in.

2. *Railroad Yard.* 1931. Gouache, 7½ x 10 in.

3. *Bridge in Jamaica, L.I.* 1931. Gouache, 7½ x 10 in.

4. *Deserted Farmhouse.* 1931. Gouache, 5½ x 8 in.

5. *Street in Brooklyn.* 1931. Gouache, 7½ x 10 in.

6. *Long Island City.* 1932. Oil, 12½ x 16½ in.

7. *Venus of 23rd Street*. 1937. Oil, 23 x 29 in.

8. *The Oculist*. 1937. Oil, 25 x 34 in.

9. *Green Cat.* 1934. Oil, 16 x 24 in.

10. *Cat Washing*. 1935. Oil, 16 x 24 in.

11. *Interior with Easel.* 1935. Oil, 12 x 20 in.

12. *Cat in Alleyway*. 1935. Oil, 16 x 32 in.

13. *Horse and Wagon.* 1935. Oil, 24 x 32 in.

14. *Union Square.* 1936. Oil, 25 x 34 in. Mr. and Mrs. Max Margulis, New York

15. *Martin Craig.* 1936. Oil, 12 x 20 in. Joseph Hirschhorn, New York

16. *Theatre*. 1936. Oil, 26 x 36 in.

17. *Madison Square Park.* 1938. Oil, 26 x 36 in. Mr. and Mrs. William Sallar, New York

18. *Ruth.* 1941. Oil, 20 x 24 in.

19. *Ave. B.* 1937. Oil, 24 x 32 in.

20. *Bootblack Shop.* 1937. Oil, 25 x 35 in.

21. *The Red Semaphore.* 1937. Oil, 26 x 36 in. Mr. and Mrs. M. Victor Leventritt, New York

22. *The Violinist.* 1937. Oil, 24 x 32 in.

23. *Demolition*. 1938. Oil, 24 x 35 in.

24. *New York Nocturne.* 1938. Oil, 26 x 36 in.

25. *East Side Playground.* 1938. Oil, 30 x 38 in.

26. *Watching an Excavation.* 1938. Oil, 30 x 36 in.

27. *Ice Cellar*. 1938. Oil, 28 x 36 in.

28. *Railroad Yard in Spokane.* 1939. Gouache, 9 x 12 in.

29. *Cherchez La Femme.* 1940. Gouache, 6 x 10 in.

30. *Tinsmith Shop.* 1940. Gouache, 11 x 13 in.

31. *Ice Cellar.* 1940. Gouache, 10 x 12 in.

32. *Furnished Room.* 1939. Oil, 16 x 24 in.

The Blue Blotter. 1939. Oil, 12 x 20 in.

34. *Self Portrait.* 1939. Oil, 12 x 20 in.
   Mr. and Mrs. Hans Moller, New York

35. *Matisse Print.* 1940. Oil, 12 x 20 in. Mr. David Liss, New York

36. *Books and Ruler.* 1940. Oil, 12 x 20 in.

37. Books and Catalogues. 1940. Oil, 18 x 18 in.

38. *The Open Window.* 1940. Oil, 12 x 20 in.

39. *Corner of a Room.* 1941. Oil, 20 x 26 in.

Loft Interior. 1941. Oil, 16 x 20 in. Mr. and Mrs. M. Margolin, Jamaica, New York

41. *Three Trees.* 1942. Oil, 16 x 24 in.

42. *Self Portrait*. 1941. Oil, 18 x 24 in.

43. *St. George Church on a Grey Day.* 1942. Oil, 12 x 20 in.
   Dr. and Mrs. Sam Prince, North Bergen, N.J.

44. *Murray Golden.* 1942. Oil, 12 x 16 in. The Phillips Gallery, Washington, D.C.

45. *Study for a portrait of Mozart.* 1944. Silkscreen, 7 x 9 in.

46. *Study for a portrait of Mozart.* 1944. Silkscreen, 7½ x 9½ in.

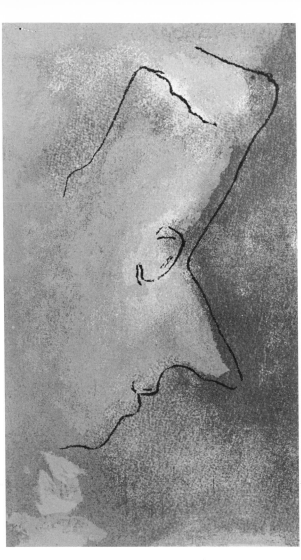

47. *Study for a portrait of Mozart.* 1944.
Silkscreen, 7 x 9½ in.

48. *Study for a portrait of Mozart.* 1944.
Silkscreen, 7½ x 8½ in.

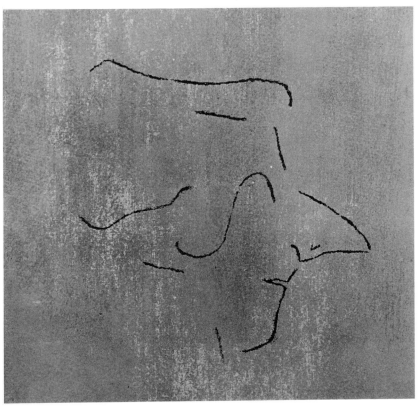

49. *Ruth and Wendy.* 1942. Oil, 12 x 20 in.

50. *Memoranda Catalogue.* 1946. Oil, 12 x 20 in. Mr. and Mrs. L. Mark, New York

51. *Teapot and Whiskbroom.* 1946. Oil, 12 x 20 in. Mr. and Mrs. Robert Benjamin, Great Neck, L.I.

52. *Window Interior*. 1947. Oil, 12 x 20 in. Mr. and Mrs. Max Margulis, New York

53. *Open Windows*. 1948. Oil, 12 x 20 in. Private collection.

54. *Regards from Chicago*. 1948. Oil, 16 x 20 in.

55. *Still Life with El Greco*. 1948. Oil, 12 x 20 in. The Phillips Gallery, Washington, D.C.

Autumn Leaves. 1950. Oil, 16 x 24 in. Mr. and Mrs. Joseph Miller, New York

57. *Broom and Teapot.* 1947. Oil, 16 x 24 in. Mr. and Mrs. E. Brown, Great Neck, L.I.

Manhattan Bridge. 1950. Oil, 24 x 30 in. Dr. and Mrs. G. Bernhardt, East Islip, L.I.

59. *The Purple Window.* 1950. Oil, 20 x 30 in. Mr. and Mrs. Edmund Weil, New York

60. *Studio Interior with Statue.* 1950. Oil, 16 x 24 in. Joseph Hirschhorn, New York

61. *Blue Statuette.* 1950. Oil, 12 x 20 in. Dr. and Mrs. G. Bernhardt, East Islip, L.I.

62. *Studio.* 1950. Oil, 12 x 20 in.

63. *Studio Interior.* 1951. Oil, 24 x 30 in. Dr. and Mrs. Sam Prince, North Bergen, N.J.

64. *Standing Figure*. 1949. Oil, 12 x 20 in.
    Private collection.

65. *Nude*. 1948. Oil, 14 x 18 in.
    Mr. and Mrs. Pinelas, New York

6. *Lying Figure.* 1948. Oil, 12 x 20 in. Mr. and Mrs. Robert Goodman, New York

67. *Light in August.* 1951. Oil, 26 x 36 in.

68. *The Broom.* 1947. Oil, 16 x 20 in. The Phillips Gallery, Washington, D.C.

69. *The Studio*. 1948. Oil, 12 x 20 in. Brandeis University Collection, Waltham, Mass.

70. *Interior with Pink Cloth.* 1951. Oil, 18 x 24 in. Whitney Museum of American Art, New York

71. *Sculptor's Stand.* 1951. Oil, 16 x 24 in. Mr. and Mrs. Berbard Green, New York

72. *Blue Statuette.* 1949. Oil, 16 x 24 in. Mr. and Mrs. J. Sabbeth, Brooklyn, N.Y.

73. *Studio.* 1950. Oil, 18 x 24 in. Dr. and Mrs. J. Mandelbaum, Brooklyn, N.Y.

74. *The Matchbox.* 1949. Oil, 16 x 20 in.

75. *Portrait of Rose.* 1950. Oil, 28 x 36 in. Mr. and Mrs. A. Bank, Pittsburgh, Pennsylvania.

76. Warren Miller. 1950. Oil, 12 x 20 in.

77. *Blue Interior.* 1951. Oil, 24 x 30 in. Mr. and Mrs. Louis Smith, New York

8. *Interior with Green Wall.* 1949. Oil, 16 x 24 in.

79. *Studio Interior*. 1950. Oil, 28 x 38 in. Mrs. Ethel Elkind, New York

80. *The Drawing.* 1948. Oil, 16 x 20 in.

81. *Juliet*. 1953. Oil, 16 x 20 in.

82. *Byron Browne.* 1954. Oil, 26 x 36 in. Joseph Hirschhorn, New York

83. *Helen.* 1951. Oil, 16 x 20 in. Mr. and Mrs. Fred Romanofsky, Long Beach, L.I.

84. *Ronni.* 1950. Oil, 24 x 30 in. Joseph Hirschhorn, New York

85. *Naomi*. 1951. Oil, 16 x 20 in. Joseph Hirschhorn, New York.

86. *Lottie.* 1954. Oil, 12 x 20 in. Mr. and Mrs. A. Altman, New York.

87. *Gwen*. 1957. Oil, 12 x 20 in. Mr. and Mrs. Bernard Cole, New York.

88. *Eddie.* 1950. Oil, 16 x 20 in. Dr. and Mrs. Fred Elias, Woodstock, N.Y.

89. *Lillian.* 1953. Oil, 12 x 20 in. Mr. and Mrs. Joseph Miller, New York

90. *Judy.* 1957. Oil, 14 x 18 in. Dr. and Mrs. Sam Prince, North Bergen, N.J.

91. *Esther.* 1955. Oil, 16 x 24 in. Dr. and Mrs. Sam Prince, North Bergen, N.J.

92. *The Artist's Mother.* 1955. Oil, 12 x 20 in.

93. *Rosemary*. 1959. Oil, 16 x 20 in.
   Mr. and Mrs. G. M. Konecky, Sands Point, L.I.

94. *Elsie Romanofsky*. 1954. Oil, 12 x 20 in.

95. Bernard. 1957. Oil, 20 x 45 in.
Mr. and Mrs. Bernard Braddon, New York

96. *Bobby*. 1958. Oil, 10 x 12 in. Mrs. Mary Miller, Brooklyn, N.Y.

97. *Jane.* 1956. Oil, 12 x 20 in. Mrs. Mary Miller, Brooklyn, N.Y.

98. *Ruth W.* 1958. Oil, 8 x 10 in.

99. Jeff in Duffel Coat. 1959. Oil, 18 x 24 in. Mr. and Mrs. Herman Shapiro, Jamaica, L.I.

100. *Edmund.* 1961. Oil, 20 x 30 in. Mr. and Mrs. Edmund Weil, New York

101. *Raphael Soyer*. 1956. Oil, 12 x 20 in.
Mr. Armand Erpf, New York

102. *William Sallar*. 1960. Oil, 12 x 20 in.
The Phillips Gallery, Washington, D.C.

103. *Helen*. 1960. Oil, 12 x 20 in.
Mr. and Mrs. Max Margulis, New York

104. *Jane*. 1953. Oil, 12 x 20 in.
Mr. and Mrs. Jack Miller, Larchmont, N.Y.

105. *Cleves Street, Rockport, Mass.* 1958. Oil, 14 x 30 in.
    Mr. and Mrs. Charles Renthal, New York

Railroad Yard, Gloucester, Mass. 1953. Oil, 18 x 24 in.

107. *Paul.* 1949. Oil, 16 x 20 in.

108. *Self Portrait.* 1956. Oil, 12 x 20 in.
Mr. Abe Lerner, New York

109. *Bottles*. 1956. Oil, 9 x 12 in.

110. *Chair and Puppet.* 1956. Oil, 14 x 18 in.

111. *Plant.* 1956. Oil, 14 x 18 in.
   Hallmark Cards Inc., Kansas City, Mo.

112. *Rosemary*. 1957. Oil, 14 x 18 in.

113. *Angela.* 1957. Oil, 18 x 24 in.

114. *Antennae*. 1957. Oil, 14 x 30 in.
Mr. and Mrs. Seymour Copstein, New York

115. *Natalie.* 1960. Oil, 28 x 36 in. Mr. and Mrs. Bernard Braddon, New York

116. *Pushcart*. 1959-60. Oil, 24 x 36 in.

117. *Miriam.* 1960. Oil, 12 x 20 in.
Mr. and Mrs. John Begg, Hastings-on-the-Hudson, N.Y.

118. *Signe*. 1960. Oil, 12 x 20 in.
   Mr. and Mrs. Waldemar Nielsen, New York

119. *Rosalind Browne.* 1958. Oil, 24 x 30 in.

120. *Mady.* 1958. Oil, 18 x 24 in. Mr. and Mrs. Marvin Kalb.

121. *Anita.* 1960. Oil, 14 x 30 in.
  Mr. and Mrs. E. Brown, Great Neck, L.I.

122. *Walter Starkie.* 1959. Oil, 24 x 30 in.

123. *Marie*. 1959. Oil, 26 x 36 in.

124. *Geri Pine*. 1960. Oil, 24 x 36 in.

125. *Andy.* 1962. Oil, 16 x 24 in.

126. *East Village Couple.* 1962. Oil, 24 x 40 in. A.C.A. Gallery, New York

127. *Margie.* 1962. Oil, 24 x 40 in. Mr. and Mrs. Irwin Corey, Great Neck, L.I.

128. *Girl from Trinidad.* 1964. Oil, 12 x 20 in.

129. *Jan.* 1962. Oil, 20 x 30 in. A.C.A. Gallery, New York

130. *Judy L.* 1962. Oil, 24 x 30 in. A.C.A. Gallery, New York

131. *Adrienne.* 1965. Oil, 12 x 20 in.

132. *Pink Slacks.* 1962. Oil, 24 x 48 in. A.C.A. Gallery, New York

133. *Paul*. 1963. Oil, 12 x 20 in.

134. *Ronni Resting.* 1961. Oil, 18 x 24 in. Mr. and Mrs. H. Rabinowitz, Brooklyn, N.Y.

135. *Pinky.* 1962. Oil, 12 x 20 in.

136. *Ronni.* 1963. Oil, 10 x 14 in.

137. *Wrap-around.* 1964. Oil, 24 x 30 in.

138. *Muriel*. 1964. Oil, 12 x 20 in. A.C.A. Gallery, New York

139. *Lynn.* 1963. Oil, 20 x 40 in.
A.C.A. Gallery, New York

140. *Seated Figure*. 1963. Oil, 26 x 36 in.
Mr. and Mrs. L. Bernstein, East Williston, L.I.